From Shannon
07/2014

ONE HUNDRED WAYS
FOR A
Chicken to Train Its
Human

D0067210

ONE HUNDRED WAYS
FOR A

Chicken to Train Its Human

BY
Diane Parker

ILLUSTRATIONS BY
Jilly Wilkinson

HODDER &
STOUGHTON

Text copyright © 2007 by Diane Parker
Illustrations copyright © 2007 by Jilly Wilkinson

First published in Great Britain in 2007

The right of Diane Parker to be identified as the Author of
the Work has been asserted by her in accordance with the
Copyright, Designs and Patents Act 1988.

11

All rights reserved. No part of this publication may be
reproduced, stored in a retrieval system or transmitted,
in any form or by any means, without the prior written
permission from the publisher, nor be otherwise circulated
in any form of binding or cover other than that in which
it is published and without a similar condition being
imposed on the subsequent purchaser.

British Library Cataloguing in Publication Data
A record for this book is available from the British Library

ISBN: 978 0 340 910207

Typeset in Baskerville by Avon DataSet Ltd,
Bidford-on-Avon, Warwickshire

Printed and bound by
CPI Group (UK) Ltd, Croydon, CR0 4YY

The paper and board used in this paperback are natural recyclable products
made from wood grown in sustainable forests. The manufacturing processes
conform to the environmental regulations of the country of origin.

Hodder & Stoughton
A Division of Hachette Children's Books
338 Euston Road
London NW1 3BH
www.madaboutbooks.com

This book is dedicated to Jupiter,
my wonderful cockerel, and to my
hens, Mercury, Venus and Saturn,
who have made sure that I keep
my place in their pecking order.

Contents

Who Rules the Roost?

Humans always think they are in charge. They sometimes refer to you by using fowl language such as 'bird brain' and 'oven-ready', but, as the saying goes, 'birds of a feather should flock together'. It's now time to give them a bit of a roasting and change the pecking order.

Showing off is a most unattractive characteristic in a human. The true meaning of 'cocksure' resides in the noble cockerel – and is a virtue. Remember this when you are strutting your stuff and crowing your heart out at dawn. Humans say that this is the best part of the day, so assist them by ensuring that you take charge of the situation; do not let them oversleep and waste the day away. They will admire your leadership skills, effective time management and concern for them and the neighbours – who can also enjoy the early part of the day with them.

Human females have hen parties. They drink excessive alcohol and make fools of themselves. You can party too and enjoy a night with the girls without getting drunk. For beauty tips for the evening, see the chapter entitled – Pullet Power.

Avoid uninvited guests, especially ones with four legs, pointy ears and a bushy tail. You do not want to get your feathers ruffled in a skirmish; your appearance and dignity are of the utmost importance. Humans are also unwelcome. Your coop is your castle, and they would probably not be interested in

your conversation about worm
length and width.

Let your feathers down and make as much noise as you like. Your clucking is well within the permitted decibel levels and your human can always catch up on sleep at another time.

Don't worry about the morning after the night before. Unmade nests, broken eggs and scattered food – your human will not even notice the difference, and they always have spare time to clean up after you.

Sometimes, small humans may come and stare at you. They have fingers that look like worms. If they poke one through the fence at you – treat it like any other worm. Try not to swallow it, though.

Remember, evolution has been good to you and dealt you a good hand. Your eggs provide unrivalled bargaining power. If your human upsets you, they may endure a long wait for breakfast.

You may want to start a family at some time. Humans are suckers for little fluffy things, and will go all silly and gaga over the sight of a mother with her chicks. They really will be putty in your wings.

Don't feel guilty; this is the right pecking order. Humans see themselves in you. After all, it's not important which came first, the chicken or the egg, is it? The point is that both came well before the human race made an appearance.

Fowl Play

It is important that your human realises that you are not just there to lay eggs. Play is important for all poultry. If you can't play in your coop – get out of it.

'Free range' means you have the right to roam. However you choose to do it, escape on a regular basis and refuse to return until you are ready.

Time in the coop should be used constructively. Providing eggs for human consumption is not your priority. Keep abreast of developments in the garden and plan ahead for trips out.

When you do manage to escape, make sure you make the best use of your time. Have a good itinerary and make sure you know your human's garden well, because that way you do not miss out on any vital areas.

Choose your times for escaping wisely. Watch what your human is doing in the garden. When they have just mowed the grass is an excellent time: firstly because it seems to tire them out, so they will be too exhausted to chase you around; and secondly because the grass cuttings are full of exciting things to eat.

A good itinerary will include the flower bed. You can really help your human by scratching out those nasty weeds that annoy them so much, and in return for this favour feel free to eat as many edible flowers as you can; after all, some plants need deadheading – even if they are not quite dead yet.

En route to your next stop, have a good scratch on the lawn; you will do your human a real favour by aerating the soil and scarifying the grass.

You will not want to miss out on the salad bed. Your human will be thrilled if you thin out the tender succulent lettuce that they are really only growing for your benefit – they always plant far too many to eat themselves.

Remember that this is only your first course, so do not over-indulge. Have another run around the garden to make room for your main course. You will find this on the compost heap – the fattest worms you could wish for. Your human will be happy that you are turning over the rotting matter and giving a new shape to their compost heap, even if you do happen to spread it all over the lawn.

For a tasty dessert, head for the bird table. Your human should be encouraged to replenish this regularly for the small garden birds, who are very careless and spill a lot of the seed onto the floor for you to pick up.

While you are out, make sure you give something back to your human to say thank you. They love chicken poo. It is the best fertiliser they can get their hands on. It is far superior to any other farmyard poo, as it is full of sulphate of ammonia, sulphur phosphate and potash; that's obviously why it smells so good.

Feel free to leave as much as you can wherever you can, even if it is all over the lawn where your humans love to walk barefoot, or even on the patio area where they have a barbecue.

They also plant things in pots just for your convenience. You can easily select what you want to eat without worrying about weeds, and it is served with a bit of style in a nice terracotta pot.

The time of year makes a difference, too, so choose your excursions wisely to gain maximum benefit from your human's hard toil in the garden.

Autumn is great. If your human has an orchard, make sure you pay a visit. Beware of the fermenting windfalls, though. This fruit is quite potent, so do not exceed your daily units of alcohol.

The day after bonfire night can be fun. Head for where they had the bonfire. There will be plenty of left-over food for you to sample, as humans are careless and drop things all the time. The ashes are fun to scratch in. Just make sure the fire has gone out first.

If you can make it as far as your human's house, you could be onto a winner. A bit of surveillance is necessary to make sure they are not around, though. If they have a cat flap, learn to use it. This will mean you have 24-hour access, to come and go as you please.

Once you get in, head for the cat or dog food. Your human will have left this on the floor just waiting for you to take it. Just make sure the cat or dog is not present while you enjoy this activity.

On your way out, make sure you wipe your feet. You don't want any germs from the dogs, cats or humans to be carried into your coop.

When you have had enough roaming for the day, make sure you only go back into your coop if your human bribes you with genuine food (even if you *want* to go back in); sometimes they will try to trick you by tapping an empty container. This is not acceptable, so if you are prepared to give up your freedom for the next few hours make sure the bribe is edible.

Don't forget: 'free range' also means varying your itinerary, however slightly, on a daily basis; otherwise your human might begin to suspect fowl play.

Feeling Peckish

Don't be fooled by your human saying it is wrong to play with your food. Everything tastes better if you scratch it, stamp on it and move it around the floor first.

Try to tip your food hopper up so that all the corn spills. That way your human will have to refill it more often.

Use your water container as a paddling pool. It's refreshing for your feet in the summer and your human will love constantly changing the water for a fresh supply.

Tip your water container up if you can; the moist soil underneath it will attract small worms to the surface for you to snack on.

Sometimes your human will offer you grit to eat. Don't be alarmed; it's just like their muesli, and it is good for you. It will aid your digestion and keep your eggshells firm.

Slugs are tasty but beware those really big ones; train your human to throw the occasional lettuce in with the nice bite-sized slugs still attached to it. That way you get your meat and vegetables in one meal.

Your human should also give you the occasional snail. They consider snails to be a delicacy and spend a fortune on them. Your meal is cheap and comes fully gift wrapped. Just make sure you remove the outer shell before tucking in.

Humans love to dine with each other, but you can do one better – dine *off* each other. If you find a willing partner, indulge in a bit of mutual grooming; whatever you find, you can eat.

Always dive back into your coop if your human is trying to clean it out, as they will unearth all sorts of lovely treats for you to enjoy in the old bedding. You can assist them by eating any flies and mites that are still clinging to your bedding.

Poultry Pals

To live in harmony with your human and other animals is important. But always remain alert, and be aware of some of the dangers that certain liaisons can bring.

The Ancient Greeks believed that even a lion was afraid of a cockerel. If you are a cockerel, keep that belief going. You are bold and brave and you have hens to protect. You were given the tools to fight with, so, if necessary, use them. You are the boss.

If you are a hen, just let the cockerel *think* he is boss. Humour him; it's good for his ego and he will protect you. After all – you know the truth.

Beware of your human's dog: he may appear to be friendly but he is probably only doing that to score brownie points with his master. Dogs are like that. Remember that anything with carnivorous teeth is a threat to you (including humans).

Never, under any circumstances, make friends with a fox.

Guard your pen with honour. Sometimes magpies will try to steal your food and eggs, so make sure they know who is boss. Assemble a crowd and mob them the minute they try anything.

Squirrels can annoy you by digging up your ground to bury nuts; however, they may be of use to you if they can unearth a worm or two. Judge each occasion separately: if it is to your advantage, let them stay; if not, see them off.

Beware of any bird of prey, especially if you are out on one of your jaunts in the garden. Your human may 'Ooh' and 'Aah' at the sight of a majestic hawk soaring overhead, but you do not want to be its next meal.

Small humans may want to pick you up. Train them not to do this by flapping your wings in their face and squawking like something possessed. If this doesn't work, poo

on them if you can. They may find this funny, but they won't when their big human tells them off for getting their clothes dirty.

A void all small humans if they are a) holding a hosepipe or b) holding a water pistol. Avoid large humans if they are a) under the influence of alcohol (this is when they are at their most stupid) or b) carrying an axe.

Eggstra special

Your eggs are a nutritious food source for billions of humans. They just can't get enough of them, and delight in collecting your freshly-laid eggs for breakfast. But you must not let them take you for granted; you are not a machine.

Make sure you get plenty of muck on your eggs; your humans love to boast and show people that they are free range. If you can get a few feathers to stick on as well, it all adds to the effect.

Lay lots of odd-shaped eggs, as humans have a strange sense of humour and even take photos of such things and then send them off to magazines for other humans to laugh at.

Sometimes you may lay an egg with a soft shell; this is quite normal, but it is great fun to watch your human as they collect it. They will be fooled by its appearance, as it usually looks like any other egg, but as they grab hold, it will disintegrate into a sticky mess in their hands.

Try to lay a double yolk occasionally – your human will be thrilled and may double your feed as a reward.

Chicken Chatter

Humans like to think that they understand what animals say. But until they are fully trained, they really haven't a clue what you are saying. So have some fun while they are learning.

Firstly, they may give you a really stupid name. You decide whether you like it. If you do, answer to it occasionally; if you don't, ignore them at all times – unless they have food.

You must train your human to know exactly what it means when the cockerel crows at dawn. Say it over and over again, as they are a bit slow first thing in the morning. As loudly as you can – 'GET UP, EVERYONE IN THE WHOLE NEIGHBOURHOOD, – *NOW*!'

The hurried clucking of a hen when laying an egg is distinctive. What you do every day is amazing; no human could even come close to what you achieve. Be proud and tell them before, during and after the activity – over and over again.

Cosy Coop

Humans are obsessed with their houses. They are always changing the carpets and decorating the walls. Within reason, you can be house-proud too. Do not allow your straw to sit still or remain fresh for too long; your human will be only too happy to change it regularly.

A comfortable perch is essential, so train your human to apply the principle that they would use when choosing a new sofa. They must bear certain things in mind, which all apply to the suitability of your perch;

- Does it fit?
- Is it too wide?
- Is it too narrow?
- Can you snuggle up for the evening next to your partner on it?

Humans like to have a well-stocked food cupboard and fridge. Do not allow them to clean your coop too regularly. Woodlice, spiders and other creepy-crawlies gather over a period of time and provide a welcome snack, particularly when you are having a night in.

Humans like a nice soft bed, so they must be trained to give you a nice nesting box to lay your eggs in. Refuse to co-operate with any egg-laying duties until you are comfortable.

While windows aren't paramount (and you do not share your human's nasty habit of staring from behind the curtains at their neighbours), good ventilation *is* important. Even a human can drill a hole for the air to get through.

Refuse to come out of your coop if there is snow on the ground. Wait until your human has laid a nice outside carpet of bedding before even considering venturing out.

Avian Attitude

Humans need to learn from your behaviour. It teaches them what makes you tick, and after extensive study they may even write books about it. Make sure you show them a rich variety of your characteristics, however frustrating your human may find them.

In summer it's lovely to enjoy the long evenings. Your human will try to shorten yours by putting you into your coop just before their favourite soap starts. Refuse to be cooped up until *you* are ready for bed.

Make sure your human provides adequate cover if they go on holiday. Your temporary chicken-sitter must be the sort that will enjoy looking after you and will feed you even more than your usual human.

If you find a good chicken-sitter, reward them by behaving. Do not escape and make them run around after you and do not fly up into their face as soon as they enter your pen.

Remember, you can go back to your normal behaviour when your usual human returns.

Try to learn a trick or two, and your human will delight in calling the neighbours round to watch. Only perform the trick if there is food involved.

Pullet Power

A pullet is a young hen. This is the time when you are at your most beautiful. You must work at it to stay looking young, as some humans are always looking for younger, more beautiful birds.

Human females put mud on their faces to keep them looking young and beautiful. They wash it off, but you don't have to. Take a regular dust bath to remove any bugs that have been there for a while. You can eat them afterwards

and your human will be envious that you can bathe and dine at the same time.

Small humans may have to see the nit nurse. For some strange reason they are horrified by this. You can elect a nit nurse from among your flock, or do it on a rota basis to inspect and eat whatever you catch.

Small humans may have a sandpit in the garden. You can have a really good makeover here; there is not much to eat, but have a good scratch around. The sand around your feet will act like a pumice stone.

Humans have to wear water-proof coats when it rains, but you don't, as your feathers have a waterproof coating. It will do your humans good if, on the odd occasion, they enjoy the feeling of rain on their skin. This will alleviate the odd smell they have. You can help them to do this by escaping the minute they are caught in a thunderstorm. They will be grateful for the invigorating exercise and the wash will do them good.

Sunlight is good for you. Humans are obsessed with getting a tan. You are far too superior for such a need. But if you can stretch your wings out in the sunshine, it will be of benefit. The vitamin D helps with your egg-laying and you can eat the toasted fly that has been stuck behind your wing as an alfresco summer treat.

Moulting is not so attractive, but it is necessary, and you can take pride that yours comes back, whereas some humans lose it for good.

Fitter Fowl

Your human is always trying out new exercises to keep fit and lose weight. You can help them by sharing some of their keep-fit regimes.

Yoga – It is important to keep supple. Encourage your human to take part in a few simple stretching positions. This will involve them standing on tiptoe and trying to get you down from the tree that you have just flown into. Ensure that all of your companions flock around them, flapping and squawking in a frenzy; your human will have to use every muscle to avoid stepping on them, and will benefit from practising their hand-and-feet co-ordination.

Aerobics – You can help your human take part in this excellent calorie-burning exercise. If your human is trying to put you to bed early, run round and round the coop flapping your wings, and don't stop till you have had enough. For some strange reason your human will follow you and mirror your actions.

Kick-boxing – As a cockerel you may need to defend your territory. This is your patch, after all. Your spurs are not just for ornament, so if your human invades your personal space, practise this ancient contact sport with them. They will appreciate your input and it will help to improve their defence mechanisms – in time.

Sprint – You may need to run very fast if your human's dog catches you stealing his food. You will be doing your human a big favour by allowing the dog to chase you back to your pen, thus giving it exercise and saving your human from having to walk it.

High jump – Remember that you are not really built for flight, so use this only if you cannot find another method of escaping from your coop for the day.

Broody and Moody

Humans think you are bird-brained or stupid. Sometimes they may not want you to sit on your eggs so that they hatch. On such occasions, don't be fooled by the underhand method of replacing your eggs with a china one. China is for tea and the 'yolk' is at your human's expense!

Use the time to meditate; breathe deeply, inhale and growl at your human if they try to move you. Show them you have the right to be moody whenever you wish. If they persist, give them a quick peck on the cheek. They will soon realise that this is not to be taken in the same manner as a human kiss. If you manage to draw blood, it will show them the pitfalls of taking on a moody female.

Hen-tertainment

Humans think that TV pro-grammes and music are only for their benefit. They may put a radio into your coop as a ploy to relax you into becoming an egg-laying zombie. But you have your needs, too. If your interests were taken into consideration by the entertainment industry, a lot of improvements could be made.

Favourite light entertainment programme – *The Eggs Factor*

Favourite song – 'I should be so clucky'

Favourite film – *Chicken Run*

Favourite news programme – *News at Hen*

Favourite soap – *East-Henders*.

There is an old saying in the entertainment industry that you should never work with children and animals. Ignore this. Small humans are much easier to extract food from as their hands have not quite mastered the grip that larger humans develop. If they enter your territory with any food in their

hands, do them a favour by reliev-
ing them of the burden. If you can
eat it – take it. Remember that
possession is 9/10ths of the law.

Chicken Wisdom

'Why did the chicken cross the road?' Do not be tempted to answer this question. It's a very old joke and in very bad taste. If you need to cross any roads, just make sure there are no humans around when you do. They think they own them, and your safety is at risk with any human behind the wheel.

Ask your human how you can be bird-brained *and* headless at the same time. Surely even with their limited intelligence they should know that this is a physical impossibility.

'The early bird catches the worm.' You need to weigh up whether you really want that extra hour in bed, or does survival of the fittest benefit a hen with insomnia?

Are legs and breasts the only meaningful criteria that some males apply for assessing feminine beauty? Cockerels need not reply as they know better.

How can humans try to lord it over chickens? Your history goes back millions of years further than theirs. Have they not heard of Chicken Supreme?

And Finally

Humans can make good pets. But it is vital that from the very start of your relationship they understand and adhere to the pecking order – YOU ALWAYS COME FIRST.